Animal Bodies

WHOSE TAIL IS THAT?

By Mary Griffin

Gareth Stevens
PUBLISHING

Please visit our website, www.garethstevens.com. For a free color catalog of all our high-quality books, call toll free 1-800-542-2595 or fax 1-877-542-2596.

Library of Congress Cataloging-in-Publication Data

Names: Griffin, Mary, 1978- author.
Title: Whose tail is that? / Mary Griffin.
Description: New York : Gareth Stevens Publishing, [2024] | Series: Animal bodies | Includes index.
Identifiers: LCCN 2022047260 (print) | LCCN 2022047261 (ebook) | ISBN 9781538286470 (library binding) | ISBN 9781538286463 (paperback) | ISBN 9781538286487 (ebook)
Subjects: LCSH: Tail–Juvenile literature.
Classification: LCC QL950.6 .G75 2024 (print) | LCC QL950.6 (ebook) | DDC 591.4–dc23/eng/20221003
LC record available at https://lccn.loc.gov/2022047260
LC ebook record available at https://lccn.loc.gov/2022047261

Published in 2024 by
Gareth Stevens Publishing
2544 Clinton Street
Buffalo, NY 14224

Designer: Tanya Dellaccio Keeney
Editor: Therese Shea

Photo credits: Cover, p. 1 KKulikov/Shutterstock.com; pp. 5, 7 Dmitriy Komarov/Shutterstock.com; pp. 9, 11, 24 Chase D'animulls/Shutterstock.com; pp. 13, 15, 24 Sanbao/Shutterstock.com; p. 17 Andrew Jeffries/Shutterstock.com; p. 19 Jim Schwabel/Shutterstock.com; pp. 21, 23 Ondrej_ Novotny_92/Shutterstock.com.

Printed in the United States of America

CPSIA compliance information: Batch #CSGS24: For further information contact Gareth Stevens, at 1-800-542-2595.

Find us on

Contents

Let's look at animal tails!
Look at this long tail.

5

It's a kangaroo.
It balances on its tail!

Look at this scaly tail.

It's a rattlesnake.
The tail's tip sounds
like a rattle!

Look at this feathery tail.

13

It's a peacock.
Its tail is longer than
its body!

Look at this powerful tail.

It's an alligator.
It uses its tail to
swim and jump!

Look at this furry tail.

21

It's a monkey.
It grabs with its tail!

23

Words to Know

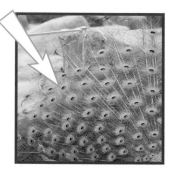
feathery

peacock

scaly

Index